CAREERS INSIDE THE WORLD OF

Homemaking and Parenting

A loving home produces a new generation of adults ready to enjoy life.

CAREERS INSIDE THE WORLD OF

Homemaking and Parenting

by Maryann Miller

THE ROSEN PUBLISHING GROUP, INC.
NEW YORK

Published in 1995 by The Rosen Publishing Group, Inc.
29 East 21st Street, New York, NY 10010

First Edition

Manufactured in the United States of America

Library of Congress Cataloging-in-Publication Data

Miller, Maryann, 1943–
    Careers inside the world of homemaking and parenting / by
Maryann Miller.—1st ed.
        p.   cm.—(Careers & opportunities)
    Includes bibliographical references and index.
    ISBN 0-8239-1901-3
1. Housewives—Vocational guidance—Juvenile literature.
2. Househusbands—Vocational guidance—Juvenile literature.
3. Parenting—Juvenile literature. [1. Housewives. 2. Househusbands.
3. Parenting. 4. Occupations.] I. Title. II. Series.
HD6073.H84M55   1994
331.7'02 — dc20   95-19045
                                                                CIP
                                                                AC

Contents

INTRODUCTION

"**I** think I want to be a lawyer," Lacy told her best friend as they finished lunch at McDonalds. "I think that would be awesome."

"Yeah, that would be great," Becky said, taking the last bite of her hamburger.

"What about you?" Lacy prodded. "What do you want to do?"

"I don't know." Becky chewed for a moment and thought about it. "I've always kind of wanted to get married and have a family."

"Wait a minute," Lacy protested. "That's not a career."

"Why not?"

"I don't know." Lacy shrugged. "Because you don't get paid for it, for one thing."

"Yeah, but think about it." Becky said. "It's a full-time job. It takes lots of work, and it's as challenging as any other job."

"And you don't get paid for it!" Lacy repeated.

"Okay. Okay. So it's not like other careers," Becky laughed, "but it is *important work*. Think

*what it would be like if we didn't have people doing
it."*

*"But they didn't have any choice in the matter.
They just did it."*

*"Maybe that's true for some," Becky said seri-
ously. "But the point is, why not think of it as a
career?"*

That's what this book is about—homemaking
and parenting as a career. It's a job people have
been doing for years without considering it a
career. As Lacy said, most people just did it. But
that has been changing.

More people, both men and women, are now
choosing full-time homemaking and parenting,
and they find the job both challenging and
rewarding.

There are some obvious differences between
these careers and any other, the major one being
that you don't get paid unless you are working
for someone else. But the importance of some
jobs can't be measured by money.

Throughout history, society has relied on the
family for strength and security. Parents guiding
their children into maturity maintain that
strength. A loving, well-adjusted home produces
a new generation of adults ready to make signifi-
cant contributions to society.

Even though the makeup of the family has
changed, the importance of family will never

Homemaking and parenting careers are both difficult and, as this mother
and son demonstrate, extremely rewarding,

change. Children who grow up in troubled homes become troubled adults. They deserve the chance to have something better.

The careers of parenting and homemaking do have some things in common with others. You have to face responsibilities, demands, and deadlines. People count on you to do your job, and meeting those challenges can be very satisfying.

There are also opportunities for paid positions in these careers. These include nannies, housekeepers, day-care workers, and au pairs. This book will introduce you to all the opportunities and help you decide if this is a career you would like to consider.

Questions to Ask Yourself

It's important to consider homemaking and parenting as serious careers. They are very different from anything else you might choose to do. 1) What makes the careers of homemaking and parenting different from other kinds of careers? 2) How are they similar to other careers? 3) What do you find most appealing about the careers of homemaking and parenting?

CHAPTER 1

WHAT IS THIS JOB?

*S*arah was baby-sitting for her older sister, Cheryl. Sarah baby-sat a lot and got along well with her niece and nephew. Usually they were ready for bed when she came, so it wasn't a big deal. But tonight Sarah had to give the kids dinner and a bath. She was pretty nervous about it.

"Don't worry," Cheryl said. "You'll do fine. The food is all ready, and the kids love their bath. They won't give you any trouble."

Sarah was relieved when the kids ate dinner with no problem. It helped that Cheryl had fixed their favorite casserole.

Bath-time turned out to be more fun than work. Sarah enjoyed playing with the kids, and their squeals of laughter made her smile.

Later, Sarah felt good sitting on the couch with a warm body snuggled on either side of her. Of course, she had to read their favorite story twice, but she

Baby-sitting can be a good start on your career as a homemaker.

didn't mind. Taking care of the children made her feel very grown-up. She wondered what it would be like to do this all the time. It was an interesting thought.

An experience like Sarah's can lead some people to consider a career as a homemaker or parent. It may even be the way most of our mothers thought about it. What is different for Sarah is that she will have more of a choice in the matter than many of our parents did.

Until recently the role of homemaker was usually filled by a woman. The husband went to work, and the wife stayed home. If they had children, the woman also cared for them. Some old **11**

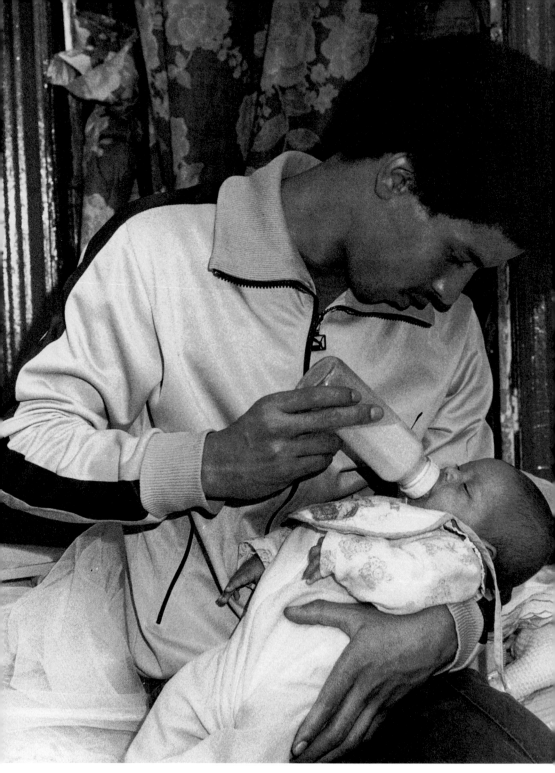

Men are taking a more active role in homemaking and parenting.

dictionaries define homemaker as "a woman who manages a home; housewife."

More current definitions include "a person who manages a household or who creates a homelike environment."

The definition has changed because the role is no longer limited to women. Men are taking a more active role in homemaking and parenting. The popular film "Mr. Mom" gave us a humorous look at the experience of a stay-at-home dad. It also showed the satisfactions and rewards.

Even dads who don't stay home all the time are more involved in child care. They help in the evenings and on weekends. Some men also take leave from their job to help with a new baby. Companies now offer family leave so that men and women can take care of the children together.

As more men are becoming more active parents, they are discovering how rewarding it is. One man thinks his decision to stay home for a year with a small child was the best thing he'd done. "It was wonderful being there and watching him grow," he says.

Another stay-at-home dad tells of his pleasure in being home with a new baby. "I was the one who noticed her first tooth. I helped her learn how to sit up, crawl, and pull herself up on the couch. It was a wonderful experience."

A person can be a homemaker without being a

parent. Single people and couples without children still have to take care of the place where they live. But you can't be a parent without being a homemaker. If you have a child, you have to have a home. It doesn't have to be a house, but it has to be a home.

Let's look at the difference in those words. A house is defined as "a structure serving as a dwelling for one or several families."

The definitions of home go much deeper. In addition to being called "a place where one lives," home is defined as "an environment or a haven of shelter, happiness, and love."

To create such an environment takes a great deal of commitment and energy.

Crossover

The careers of homemaking and parenting have some things in common. The routine tasks of cleaning and cooking, for example, have to be done in either role. You also have to do laundry even without children. There is just less to do.

Other tasks like shopping, paying bills, and maintenance have to be done in homes with no children. Therefore, combining the careers doesn't necessarily double the work.

Parenting does, however, have some added responsibilities. Those responsibilities could be broken down like this:

Parenting has added responsibilities, such as making time for doctor's appointments.

Physical care—feeding, clothing, bathing, cleaning up after.

Emotional care—talking, playing, teaching, guiding, loving.

Time demands—doctor appointments, school functions, sports, transportation.

We shall look at each of these areas in more detail.

Questions to Ask Yourself

Men and women both are beginning to choose careers for themselves as homemakers. The idea of creating a home for someone can be very appealing, whatever your sex. 1) What is the difference between homemaking and parenting? 2) How have the roles of men and women changed in homemaking and parenting? 3) Besides "Mr. Mom," what are some movies or TV programs that show men in traditionally women's roles?

CHAPTER 2

PREPARATION

Despite the fact that parenting and home-making are very important jobs, little formal education has been offered. Most people learned from their own parents, and girls could take homemaking classes in high school.

Most classes lasted only one semester, which made it difficult to learn much about being a homemaker or parent. "All I can remember is making cookies and sewing an apron," one woman said about her class in the '60s.

The good news is that high school home-making courses have changed. Some of them introduce students to child care, family problem-solving, and financial management.

College courses have changed, too. Instead of focusing on just the basics of cooking, sewing, and decorating, they cover such courses as Child Development and Parenting and also Relationships.

On the chalkboard:
screaming baby   Days to
baby waking up frequently   graduation
embarassing "mom"
boyfriend thinks "he" is right
parents yell in front of partner
mom yells when it isnt your fault
someone telling me want to do
lies to me
talking behind back   Someone tells me how I feel it isnt true
Someone takes something w/o asking

There are now college courses in Child Development and Parenting.

Another major change in homemaking courses is that they are no longer primarily for girls. Almost 42 percent of the students taking them in the '90s are boys. Boys are also joining the Future Homemakers of America. Nick Rhoton, who attends a high school in Virginia, is the current president of the club. "Males are realizing their roles in society," he says. "Everyone is a homemaker. Everyone will run a home."

Other courses are available to prepare you for the role of homemaker or parent or both:

18   **Parenting.** Take child psychology courses in

high school and college. General psychology and sociology would also be useful.

Some colleges offer continuing education courses in parenting. Similar programs are also offered through schools and churches.

Homemaking. Time-management courses would be helpful for planning and efficiency. Handling family finances would be easier after taking some money-management classes. Courses in repairs and home maintenance are usually available through continuing education or recreation programs.

Educate Yourself

You don't have to rely on courses to prepare for a career as a homemaker or parent. Books about parenting and homemaking are in most libraries. You can also find books on finances, home repair, and other "how-to" subjects.

A book that offers a simple approach is John Rosemond's *Six-Point Plan for Raising Happy, Healthy Children.* Rosemond believes that good parenting "comes from the heart and the gut. It is not a matter of long, hard thought, but a matter of how sensitive you are to *your* needs and the needs of your child, and how firmly grounded you are in the soil of common sense."

Before Karen became a parent, she thought she was well prepared. She had been around children

*most of her life, and she'd even studied child psy-
chology in college. But all of a sudden her three
children were out of control. Bobby had stopped
making good grades in school. Melissa sulked all
the time, and Jeremy was hitting other kids.*

*Karen started looking for solutions in books and
articles about parenting. What she found was contradictory. She wasn't sure what to act on. She
was also feeling less sure of herself as a parent.*

*"I finally realized that it had to stop," Karen
says. "If you lose your confidence as a parent, you
will have a tougher time of it."*

*Karen decided to rely on her common sense.
From all the advice, she used only what she
believed was best. "It didn't make the problems go
away," she says. "But it helped me find the solutions that worked best for my family."*

The fact that Karen continued to educate herself is important here. As Julie Ross writes in
Practical Parenting for the 21st Century, "Pure in-
stinct is not enough for effective parenting. We
educate ourselves for every other job we hold in
society. Being a parent shouldn't be the excep-
tion. Our children's futures are too important to
leave to chance."

Go to the Source

Another way to find out more about homemaking
and child care is to talk to people who are doing

Parents are always learning about their career, from other parents and from people who have no children.

the jobs. Your own parents would be a good first source. Then talk to young parents, single parents, and people who have no children. Ask them how they handle their responsibilities.

Some other good questions to ask are:

- What are the best things about being a home-maker/parent?
- What are the worst things?
- Did you manage another career in addition to homemaking/parenting? How did you do it?
- Did you take time away from another career to be a full-time homemaker/parent? What are the advantages and disadvantages of doing that?
- What are the most important things to consider in deciding to have a child?

Keep in mind that both careers are full of surprises. The ability to be flexible and adapt to the unexpected will give you a better chance for success.

Questions to Ask Yourself

Neither homemaking nor parenting is an easy job. Both require a lot of preparation and common sense. 1) What courses can you take in school to help you prepare for a career in homemaking or parenting? 2) What can you do on your own to help you prepare for a career in homemaking or parenting? 3) Whom can you talk to in order to learn more about homemaking and parenting?

CHAPTER 3

A DAY IN THE LIFE OF A HOMEMAKER

If your mom is a full-time homemaker, have you ever thought about what she does all day? Do the clean clothes magically appear in your room every week? What happens to the dust in the living room? Who pays the bills so the lights don't get turned off?

You may think those questions are silly. But some young people haven't been actively involved in housekeeping with their parents, so they don't know what is involved.

The following are the basic responsibilities:

Cleaning. Routine jobs like dusting, vacuuming, cleaning the bathroom, sweeping, cleaning appliances, washing dishes. Also periodic jobs like washing windows, cleaning closets, washing curtains, shampooing carpeting and furniture, cleaning walls and baseboards.

Laundry. Sorting, washing, drying, folding,

23

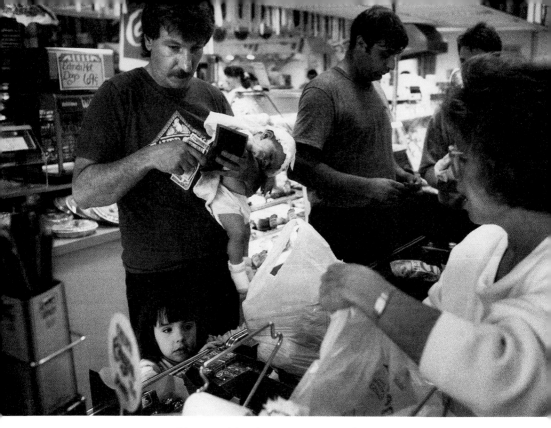

Homemaking is not an easy task.

and putting away clothes. Taking other clothes to the cleaners and picking them up.

Shopping. Planning meals and making a list of items needed. Taking an inventory of other items needed such as paper products and soap products. Going to the store, then putting everything away.

Cooking. Preparing meals that meet nutritional needs; preparing for special occasions such as holidays and guests.

Maintenance/yardwork. Home repairs, painting, lawn mowing, trimming, edging, watering, weeding, planting, clean-up.

Financial. Planning a budget, paying bills, handling insurance, investments, and savings.

Seeing it all listed together like that is almost enough to make you want to run for cover. That's an awful lot of work! How would I manage it?

The Dreaded "O" Word

The key to getting jobs done in any career is *organization*. A person has to come up with a plan to get things done and meet deadlines. It is the same with homemaking.

People who accomplish a lot make a plan for the jobs. In *Sidetracked Home Executives*, Pam Young and Peggy Jones offer a detailed plan. They suggest looking at each room and writing down what has to be done, then assigning each job a time. For instance:

BEDROOM
    Make bed—daily
    Dust—weekly
    Vacuum—weekly
    Change sheets—weekly
    Clean drawers and closets—monthly
    Wash windows—monthly
    Clean cobwebs—monthly

Make a similar list of jobs for each room of the house. Then the authors suggest writing the

Homemaking often involves a lot of cooking.

jobs on index cards and filing them according to when the job should be done. Each day do the daily jobs, then pick some from the weekly and monthly files to do.

This is a good plan, but not everybody likes that kind of organization.

Marie keeps her house clean by having a weekly cleaning session. Everybody in the family participates. Marie makes a list of jobs, and each person chooses one. As jobs are finished, others are chosen until all the jobs are done.

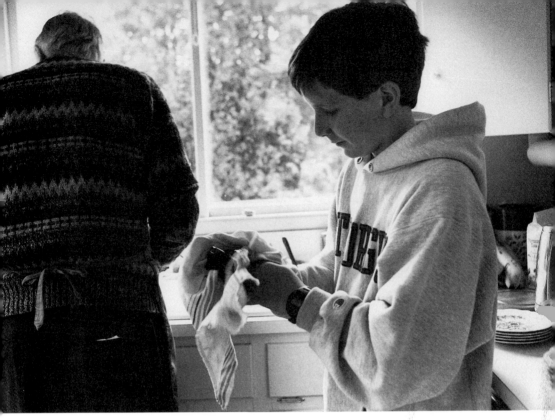

Taking care of a home can be a family team effort.

Everyone is responsible for making their own bed. The other daily chores are done on a rotating basis. Most of the time, Marie and her husband take turns cooking.

"We like not having a strict plan we have to follow," Marie says. "It lets us schedule the jobs around our activities and interests. I think our approach also works because everyone is involved. Nobody can whine and say they do more than the rest of the family."

Marie has another job outside the home, but her approach is shared by a full-time homemaker in Colorado. "I told my family if there are six people messing up a house it shouldn't be one person's responsibility to clean it up," Cleo says. Everyone in Cleo's family cleans their own room. Meal preparation and clean-up are a team effort, and everyone helps with the laundry. Larger cleaning jobs are also a group effort, including yardwork. "This is a great arrangement for a family," Cleo says. "It gets the work done, and we spend more time together. Sometimes it's more fun than work."

The Upside

Being a full-time homemaker has a number of advantages. You decide how and when things will be done. Having that kind of control over your job can be very satisfying. It gives you freedom that you don't have in other positions.

Questions to Ask Yourself

Just like every other career, there are certain responsibilities and tricks to being successful in homemaking and parenting. It's important to know what these are before starting on your career. 1) What are some basic responsibilities of housekeeping? 2) What is the key to getting jobs done in any career? 3) What are some advantages of being a full-time homemaker?

CHAPTER 4

A DAY IN THE LIFE OF A PARENT

"We grow our first and our deepest roots within family and home; strong positive feelings about ourselves and firm emotional ties to others will anchor us in life, nourish our security, and permit us to weather successfully the adversities of our lives."
—Bruno Bettelheim, *A Good Enough Parent.*

Family is no longer defined as "a mother, a father, and children." There are single-parent families, blended families, and families with no children.

A high divorce rate has increased the number of single parents, most of whom are women.

The role of a single parent is particularly hard. Many single moms have no financial or emotional support from their former husband. Most of them work at another full-time job,

29

A high divorce rate has increased the number of single families.

which limits their time with their children.

There has also been an increase in remarriage and blended families. Living in harmony in a blended family or stepfamily is not as easy as it looks on the TV show "The Brady Bunch." Jealousy and resentment can cause serious problems.

The success of parenting in any situation requires a commitment of time and self. Each parent has to answer the question, "How much of myself am I willing to invest in family life?"

Responsibilities

Parents have to take care of the physical and
emotional needs of their children. Most parents

find the physical needs easier to meet. Those needs include feeding, clothing, providing a home and transportation, and educational and medical considerations.

Meeting those needs can be physically tiring, but they are less challenging than the emotional needs of children. Defining that challenge, John Rosemond puts it in simple terms: "The purpose of raising children is simply to help them out of our lives and into successful lives of their own."

Stated that way it sounds easy, but to achieve that goal a parent must help the child attain:

- Independence
- Responsibility
- Emotional stability
- Confidence
- Self-control

Parents do this by satisfying the basic emotional needs of their children. In *Raising Kids in a Changing World* Dian Smith lists those needs as:

Love—Children need to know that they are important and someone cares for them. They should be loved and appreciated for who they are, not what they do. This builds self-esteem and confidence.

Security—Children need to believe that someone will take care of their physical and emo-

tional needs. They also need to know that someone will protect them from harm. They need to
feel safe.

Continuity—Children need things they can
count on. Some of those things include routines,
traditions, holiday celebrations, and time spent
together on a regular basis. They also need to
know what they can and cannot do, as well as what
is expected of them.

Communication—Children need to be
heard. They need to know that their ideas and
concerns are important. They need to talk to
someone who understands and accepts them no
matter what outrageous thing they say.

Identity—Children need to feel proud of who
they are. They also need to be encouraged to find
their individual gifts and talents.

Belonging—Children need to feel that they
are part of a group that can provide support and
guidance. This need can first be met in the
family, but it extends outside the home. Parents
can encourage their children to join school, com-
munity, or church organizations.

Respect—Children need to be treated with
respect. This helps them feel secure in their
identity and also teaches them respect for others.

Questions to Ask Yourself

It's not easy to be a parent. There is a lot of responsibility involved in keeping a child healthy

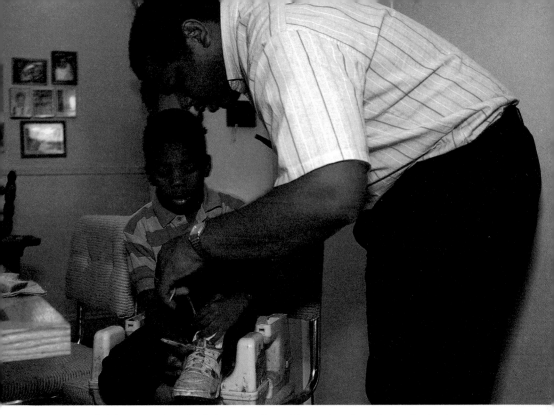

Children need to feel the security of knowing that their physical and emotional needs are being met.

and happy. 1) What are some different kinds of families? 2) What are the responsibilities a parent has to his or her children? 3) What makes someone a good parent?

CHAPTER 5

PARENTING IN ACTION

*A*ngie is a single mother with three children, ages nine, six, and three. Because of the divorce, her children have needed a great deal of extra emotional care. That has been difficult, however, because of the demands on her of working, going to school, and taking care of the home.

Aware of the need for stability and security, Angie has tried to keep their lives much the same as before. When she had to move, she made arrangements to keep the children in the same school.

Angie constantly reassures the children that she will not leave, and she gives them plenty of affection. To help build their sense of identity, she tells each of them how special they are every day. She also makes extra efforts to let them take part in activities they enjoy.

Despite their difficulties, there is a lot of laughter in Angie's home. She delights in her children, and **34** they thrive on her love. "That makes me sound like a *perfect mother,"* Angie says, *"and I'm not. Believe me. There are lots of times I lose it. There are times I get so terribly tired and wish I didn't have to do everything. But then I realize that this is what it's all about. Accepting responsibility. I gave these children life, so I can also give them the best chance of living that life to the fullest."*

Is Loving Them Enough?

No, not unless you want your child to grow up totally self-absorbed. A good parent balances love and discipline. No other area of parenting is so often misunderstood as discipline.

Discipline should not be confused with punishment. People used to think that spanking was discipline. It's *not*. Discipline is "training that develops self-control, character, orderliness, and efficiency."

When a parent disciplines a child, it's not just to make the child behave at the moment. It is to teach the child how to behave for a lifetime.

How parents discipline children has to do with parenting style. A sociologist defines three categories most American families fall into:

Authoritarian—Parents have the most power. They dictate what children will do.

Permissive—Children have the most power. They dictate what they will do and sometimes what the parent will do.

How parents discipline a child depends on their parenting style.

Authoritative—Parents have ultimate power, but children are part of the decision-making process.

Experts agree that families need rules and children need guidance. If that can be the situation in a home where there is mutual respect, it is more effective.

The whole point of discipline is to set limits. This can be done through education, example, encouragement, cooperation, and firmness. Punishment may be necessary, but it does not

have to be physical.

Many parents share care of the kids.

Family and Work

Many parents face the question of who will be
the primary caregiver for the children. More
women today work outside the home than ever
before. That raises concerns about child care and
who carries the load at home.

*John and Christy have two little girls; one is five,
the other eighteen months old. For the past couple of
years, John and Christy have shared the responsibility of caring for the children. "We did it mainly
because we didn't want someone else raising our
kids," John says. "We think it's important that kids
be at home with parents."*

*Three days a week, John works twelve-hour days.
The other four days, he takes care of the girls while
Christy works. This arrangement has met with mixed
reactions from friends and family. "The older generation think it's great," John says. "People our age
think it's crazy. Some of them don't understand why
I don't just put the girls in day care and take advantage of the free time. But I guess it's hard to understand unless you've done it."*

*John doesn't just sit at home with the kids. Once a
week he plans a special outing with them. He also
gets together with a neighbor who has young children.
That way the girls are learning to get along with
others in a group.*

*John says he doesn't regret his decision for a
minute. He knows he is raising his children the way
he wants them to be. He also finds it very satisfying*

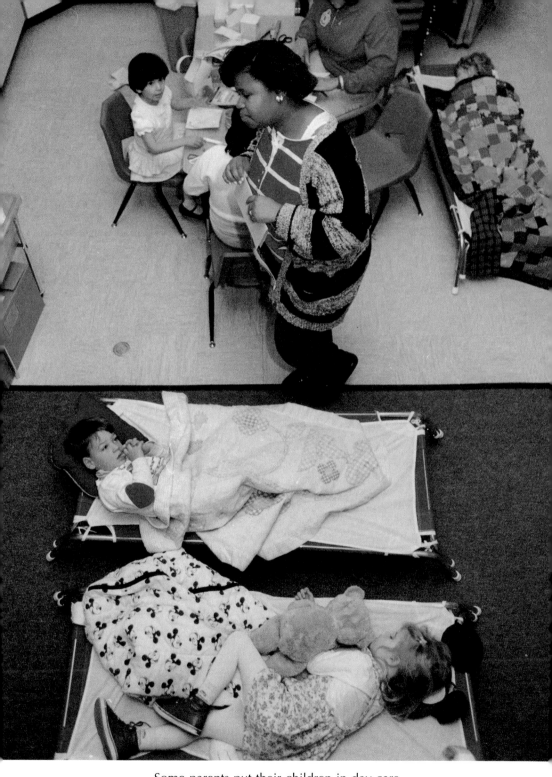

Some parents put their children in day care.

to watch the children grow and learn. "I would definitely recommend it," he says.

To Work or Not to Work

Some people believe that one parent should stay at home with the children all the time, and most experts agree that it is very important for at least the first year. That should always be taken into consideration in making the decision about work.

But more often than not there is no real choice in the matter. Survival often dictates that both parents work. Many parents do not have an option. What do you do then?

You make the best decision you can about day care. Visit the facilities. Talk to the teachers and administrators. Talk to the children and their parents. Let your children visit the center and see if they are happy there.

Then you make the best of your time with your children. People like Angie have managed to be good parents even if their time is limited. You can, too.

Questions to Ask Yourself

Parents have to make many difficult choices about the upbringing of their child. No one way is perfect; however, there is usually one way that is best for your family. 1) What style of parenting do you think is best? Why? 2) Would you want to work outside the home? Why?

CHAPTER 6

IS THIS JOB FOR ME?

It doesn't take a superhero to be a homemaker or a parent. But the jobs are easier if you have a few special characteristics. It helps to have a lot of patience and a good sense of humor. It also helps if you work well without supervision and are a self-starter.

Since parents are a child's first teachers, being persuasive and creative helps. Some parents also teach their kids at home instead of sending them to regular school. To do that takes an extra measure of patience and creativity in addition to good planning skills and a lot of preparation.

Knowing how to handle stress is important. Parents need to take time for themselves regularly. They also need to plan time just to have fun with the children and enjoy their company.

Bill and Cathy used to have a regular skip day with their two children. Once every three or four months Bill and Cathy would take a day off from work and keep the kids out of school. They'd spend the entire day just talking, laughing, and playing. "It was great," Cathy says. "It gave us all a chance to grow closer together."

Making the Decision

One way to test whether you'd even like to try one of these jobs is to list the good and bad points:

HOMEMAKING

Good Points	*Bad Points*
Be own boss	Work is never done
Set own hours	Unplanned interruptions
Choose what jobs to do when	Role not valued by others

PARENTING

Good Points	*Bad Points*
Experience the miracle of life	Constant demands
Have someone else to love	Getting up at night
Pride in what child accomplishes	Disappointments
Sharing good times	Unexpected emergencies
Growing in friendship	Conflict

Other questions to ask yourself: Do I like to cook and clean? Do I enjoy babies, children?

Do I get frustrated easily? Do I mind sharing?

Before you decide to be a parent, read the book *Test Your Parenting Potential* by William Gerin, PhD, and Jim Johnson, PhD. The book has a number of quizzes you can take to see if being a parent is what you want to do.

The quizzes help you plan ahead: How are you going to share the responsibilities of child care with your husband or wife?

The best way to do this is by discussing it with your partner and making a decision that is right for you. Maybe you will not have an equal split. Maybe roles will be reversed. But each couple have to do what they want, not what people expect of them.

Tim and Vicki have reversed the roles. She is an attorney and earns the primary income. Tim stays home and takes care of the house. He also works in a home office as a writer.

"Some of my friends think it's strange," Tim says. "But we talked about this for a long time, and we're both comfortable with the arrangement."

What does it cost to have and raise a child?

In *Children: To Have or Have Not?* Diane C. Elvenstar has a chapter that gives the details from pregnancy through college:

From birth through age 1, you will spend $5,500.

At age 5, you will spend $6,500 per year.
At age 11, you will spend $10,750 per year.
At age 16, you will spend $17,800 per year.
College costs range between $20,000 and
$30,000.
Weddings about $7,000 for a girl, $2,500 for a
boy.

These cost estimates cover food, housing, clothing, medical, dental, entertainment, and other expenses. The actual costs could be higher or lower, depending on your lifestyle and expectations. However, the costs do not double with another child.

The decision to have a child is one of the most important ones you will ever face. It should not be taken lightly or left to chance. Parents who choose to have children usually are better prepared to accept all the responsibilities. They are also happier and tend to do better than parents who are forced into the role.

Questions to Ask Yourself

Before you make the decision to be a parent, think about these questions. They might help you to prepare yourself. 1) What are some good characteristics for a parent to have? 2) What do you think are the good points of homemaking and parenting? 3) Do you think you would be a good parent or homemaker?

CHAPTER 7

SUCCESS / REWARDS

The rewards for homemaking and parenting are much different from those of other careers. You don't get a paycheck. There is no bonus plan. You don't get to dress up and go to important meetings. And you don't get vacation days and sick days.

So why do it? Because it is important work. Many of our social problems can be directly linked to family problems.

Some people choose to be a homemaker or a parent or both because doing the job well can give enormous personal satisfaction. A homemaker can take great pride in creating a warm, loving environment. Parents can take great pride in seeing their children grow into mature, healthy, interesting people.

Many parents put their success in child-rearing   **45**

above all others. A successful journalist in St. Louis puts it this way: "I've done a lot in my life that some people might envy. I've worked at high-profile, high-paying jobs, known athletic success, graduated from prestigious schools. But when I think of my achievements, I don't think of these things. I think of my sons."

A father who took a leave from his other job to help raise his kids has this to say, "The six months of my personal leave were the most productive and happiest of my life. Now when I come home from work at night, I feel like a real dad, not just a visitor."

A mother makes this comment, "Although I don't receive a salary, I consider my career one of the most satisfying, fulfilling, and at times most stressful jobs in society. Homemaking is an exciting and rewarding job and should be viewed as more than a leave of absence from society."

Another journalist who was a full-time mother first puts it this way, "There are more instant and obvious rewards from being a lawyer, or an astronaut, or a business executive, and we mothers aren't often that lucky. The pay is lousy and the only notoriety we can expect is to be taken to school for show-and-tell if we have an interesting hobby. But after investing almost seventeen years in the career, I'm beginning to see the first fruits of my efforts unfolding. Believe me, it was worth the wait."

Outside Influence

Other attitudes about full-time homemaking or parenting are not always so positive. Some people still think the careers are a terrible waste of time and talent, especially for women.

Before there were equal rights for women, many of them were trapped in roles of wife and mother. Now they have more freedom of choice. Some people think women shouldn't choose domestic careers, that by doing so they are taking a step backward.

This makes it more difficult for young people who are facing choices. One teen surprised her mother by saying she wasn't sure she wanted to go to college. "Why not?" the mother asked.

"I'm not sure I ever really wanted to do that. I just thought I had to. People have been telling me to plan big things for my life. No one told me I could be a wife and mother if I want."

Your choice about your career should be based on what you really want to do, not on what someone else thinks you should do.

If you do choose parenting or homemaking, you will have to find your own rewards. How well you do this will depend on your attitude.

As a homemaker you will spend many hours cleaning a house that only gets dirty again. As a parent, you will spend endless energy raising a child who may not end up as your pride and joy.

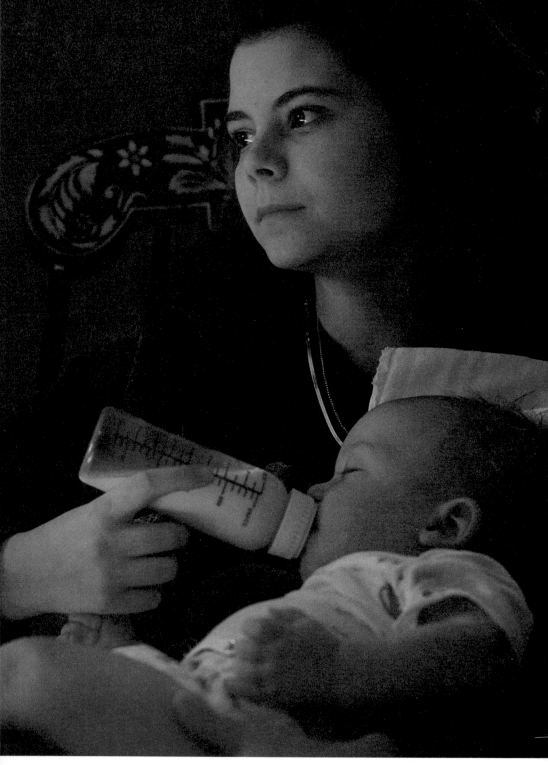

Parenting can be difficult and tiring, but it can also be worth it.

To avoid stress and burnout, psychologists recommend the following:

- Believe in yourself and your ability.
- Find something positive in your job everyday.
- Arrange time just for yourself.
- Join or start a support group.
- Maintain a sense of humor.

One mother believes that laughter is one of the best tools she has. "It can change a lot of situations," she says. "Say, for instance, you're going head to head with your thirteen-year-old son who is trying to intimidate you with his macho stance. So you turn it into a joke. You smile and tell him he is not going to get his way no matter how much he narrows his eyes and glares at you. Then you gently tease him out of his anger and pretty soon you are both laughing.

"You've still gotten your point across, and you both end up feeling good about the resolution."

The value of laughter is that it is so uplifting. It makes it easier to face the frustrations and demands of any job.

Questions to Ask Yourself

You have to make the choice of which career to follow. Think before you choose. Make sure it's *your* decision, and not anyone else's. 1) Why do you want to be a parent or homemaker? 2) What are "outside influences"? 3) How might outside influences affect your decisions in life?

CHAPTER 8

OTHER OPPORTUNITIES

You can also be a professional in these fields by working for someone else. Private Household Worker is a title given to people who provide services for other people. They generally clean homes, care for children, plan and cook meals, and do laundry.

Au pairs receive room and board in exchange for housekeeping or caring for children. They are often young people from other countries.

Houseworkers do only household cleaning.

Child-care workers care for children, wash their clothes, and clean their rooms.

Nannies care for young children.

Tutors or **Governesses** look after older children, help them with schoolwork, and may teach a foreign language.

Companions or **Personal attendants** care
50   for elderly or disabled people. They help with

bathing and dressing, prepare and serve meals, take them on outings and to appointments.

Homes with a large staff of household workers may include a **housekeeper** and a **butler**. They hire, supervise, and coordinate the work of the household staff. Butlers greet guests, answer phones, deliver messages, serve food and drinks. A butler may also drive the car and act as a personal attendant.

Cooks plan and prepare meals, clean the kitchen, order groceries and supplies.

Caretakers do heavy household work and general home maintenance.

Most household workers live in their own home and travel to work. The job requires no special training.

Special schools for nannies, butlers, housekeepers, and governesses teach household administration, bookkeeping, early childhood education, nutrition, and child care.

Private household workers can move into similar jobs in hospitals, hotels, and restaurants. The pay is usually better, and companies offer benefits such as medical insurance.

Most household workers work part time, less than 35 hours a week. Earnings vary from $10 an hour in a large city to minimum wage in other areas. Travel expenses to and from work are usually paid, and the worker receives a free meal.

Live-in workers earn more and receive free room and board. They also usually work longer hours and are limited in their contact with friends and relatives. In 1990 the average pay was $110 to $226 per week. The top 10 percent earned $290 a week or more.

Most live-in housekeepers or butlers, nannies, and governesses earn higher wages. Trained nannies in New York City can start at $250 to $450 per week and go as high as $800 per week.

Most private household workers have no health insurance, retirement plans, or unemployment compensation.

Child Care

Caring for other people's children is a good way to have an income and be at home with your own children. It also fills a great need.

Most people who provide at-home care earn between $3 and $5 an hour per child. The rate depends on how much care the child needs and what other services are provided. For after-school care, some people will take a child to athletic practices or other scheduled activities.

Caring for infants and toddlers at home can be very time-consuming. Some people even offer structured learning activities similar to a preschool. The charge for this is higher than for basic child care.

A person can also be licensed to run a day-

Instead of having kids of your own, you can work at a day care center.

care center at home. Each state regulates day-care centers.

Another option in day care is to work for an established center. Entry-level positions pay a little more than minimum wage. The responsibilities include watching the children during play-time and assisting the teachers.

To move into a higher-paying position requires more education and experience. In most centers, teachers have to have a degree in early education. Degrees in psychology and business would qualify you for a position as a director or manager.

Other

Some jobs in hotels and on cruise ships are related to "domestic services." A valet, for instance, assists guests with personal needs.

To work in a hotel or on a cruise ship, training is required. Universities that offer programs in hotel and restaurant management usually offer training in housekeeping and valet positions.

Questions to Ask Yourself

Sometimes paid jobs in the field of homemaking and parenting are the best option. They provide experience for later on, and also give an idea of what the field is really about. 1) What paid jobs using homemaking and parenting skills are available? 2) What kind of training is available for these jobs?

CHAPTER 9

HOW DO I START?

Get involved at home. Ask your parents to teach you more about running a household. Plan meals and shop together. Take turns cooking. Baby-sit. Take child-care classes. Work in the church nursery or at a day-care center.

Keep in mind, however, that no career choice has to be final. Many people change careers, blend careers, or start a new career.

One advantage of this career is that you have options. You can work at another career at home. You can start another career after your children are grown. Or you can plan for one by going to school.

Questions to Ask Yourself

If you think you might be interested in a career in homemaking, get a head start. 1) What is a good way to begin learning the skills? 2) What is one advantage of starting with a career in home-making or parenting?

Homemaking and parenting can be careers full of rewards.

GLOSSARY

adversities Problems, misfortune, bad luck.

authoritarian Favoring absolute obedience to authority, against individual freedom.

authoritative Coming from proper authority.

budget Plan of how to balance income and spending.

contradictory Saying the opposite of a statement; inconsistent.

dictate To issue orders or commands.

domestic Pertaining to family or home.

homemaker Person who manages a household.

parent Person who has the responsibility of raising a child.

permissive Not strict, allowing freedom to act in a manner of a child's own choosing.

APPENDIX A

Organizations that Support Parenting

Fatherhood Project
C/O Families and Work Institute
330 7th Avenue
New York, NY 10001
212-268-4846 Fax: 212-465-8637

Miss Mom/Mister Mom
535 Oliver Street
Moab, UT 84532
801-259-5090

Mothers at Home
8310-A Old Courthouse Road
Vienna, VA 22182
703-827-5903

Mothers Matter
171 Wood Street
Rutherford, NJ 07070
201-933-8191

**National Association of Mothers' Centers
(NAMC)**
336 Fulton Avenue
Hempstead, NY 11550
516-486-6614

Parents Without Partners
8807 Colesville Road
Silver Spring, MD 20910
301-588-9354

Single Mothers by Choice
P.O. Box 1642, Gracie Square Station
New York, NY 10028
212-988-0993

Women on Their Own
P.O. Box 1026
Willingboro, NJ 08046
609-871-1499

Center for the Study of Parent Involvement
JFK University
370 Camino Pablo
Orinda, CA 94563
510-254-0110

APPENDIX B

Legal Rights of Parents and Children

Parents have the legal right to custody of their children. They have a duty to provide food, shelter, clothing, and medical attention until the children are of age.

Parents are also responsible for the behavior of their children. They can be held liable for harm caused by their children.

Parents have the right to the services of a child living with them, including earnings.

Children are free from the legal ties to their parents when they become adults; when they enter military service; or when parent and child agree that the child is able to support himself.

Children who run away can be arrested, returned home, or placed in foster care.

Children also have legal rights. Parents cannot physically abuse or neglect their children.

Children have the right to an education. If a parent interferes with this right, authorities can **60** take action.

FOR FURTHER READING

Bacharach, Bert. *How to Do Almost Everything.*
New York: Simon & Shuster, 1970.

Bettelheim, Bruno. *A Good Enough Parent.* New
York: Alfred A. Knopf, 1987.

Birk, Gordon. *Responsibilities of Parenthood.* Balti-
more: Media Materials, Inc., 1986.

Bracken, Peg. *I Hate to Housekeep Book.* New
York: Harcourt Brace & World, 1962.

Button, Alan DeWitt. *The Authentic Child.* New
York: Random House, 1969.

Elvenstar, Diane C. PhD. *Children—To Have or
Have Not? A Guide to Making and Living with
Your Decision.* San Francisco: Harbor Publish-
ing, 1982.

Gerin, William, & Johnson, Jim. *Test Your
Parenting Potential.* New York: Prentice-Hall
Press, 1986.

Gordon, Thomas. *P.E.T.—Parent Effectiveness
Training.* New York: Peter H. Wyden, Inc.,
1970.

Guarendi, Raymond N. *You're A Better Parent*

Than You Think: A Guide to Common-Sense Parenting. Englewood Cliffs: Prentice-Hall, 1985.

Rosemond, John. *Six-Point Plan for Raising Happy, Healthy Children.* Kansas City, MO: Andrews and McMeel, 1989.

Shield, Renee Rose. *Making Babies in the '80s: Common Sense for New Parents.* Harvard and Boston: Harvard Common Press, 1983.

Smith, Dian G. *Raising Kids in a Changing World.* New York: Prentice-Hall, Press, 1991.

INDEX

ABOUT THE AUTHOR

Maryann Miller has been published in numerous magazines and Dallas newspapers. She has served as editor, columnist, reviewer, and feature writer. Currently she works as an office manager for a book distributor in Dallas.

Married for over twenty-nine years, Ms. Miller is the mother of five children. She and her husband live in Omaha, Nebraska.

Cover Photo: © Maria Taglienti/Image Bank

PHOTO CREDITS: p. 2, 11, 33, 53 © Hazel Hankin/Impact Visuals; p. 8 © Michael Kamber/Impact Visuals; p. 12 © Katherine McGlynn/Impact Visuals; p. 15, 24 © Piet van Lier/Impact Visuals; p. 18 © Evan Johnson/Impact Visuals; p. 21 © Jane Schreibman/Impact Visuals; p. 26 © Jim West/Impact Visuals; p. 27 © Catherine Smith/Impact; p. 30 © Linda Eber/Impact Visuals; p. 33 Harvey Finkle/Impact Visuals; p. 36 Andrew Lichtenstein/Impact Visuals; p. 37 © M. Brodskay/Impact Visuals; p. 39 © AP/Wide World; p. 48 © Dick Doughty/Impact Visuals; p. 56 © Sharon Stewart/Impact Visuals

PHOTO RESEARCH: Vera Ahmadzadeh with Jennifer Croft

DESIGN: Kim Sonsky